Regional American Stories, written with style and verve, have been especially selected to reflect the American way of life by centering on real people and places from definite times in history. Based on true incidents, each story brings vitally to life concepts and understandings that children need to develop about all parts of the country. Regional differences help children to better understand how others live, to appreciate their own heritage, and to develop more respect for all ethnic backgrounds.

Colorful characters and unusual events are woven into these educating stories to provide pleasure reading and to give the older child a more meaningful background in American history.

Home Is Over the Mountains

The Journey of Five Black Children

BY JAMES STREETER

ILLUSTRATED BY VICTOR MAYS

GARRARD PUBLISHING COMPANY
CHAMPAIGN, ILLINOIS

*In Memory of the Reverend James Streeter
and Tanna Streeter, my
parents, with love*

Copyright © 1972 by James Streeter
All rights reserved. Manufactured in the U.S.A.
International Standard Book Number: 8116–4256–9
Library of Congress Catalog Card Number: 70–181763

Contents

1. A Hug for Pa 7
2. Run! 15
3. On Our Own 24
4. The Dangerous Journey 33
5. Winter Camp 42
6. We Must Go East 50
7. Together at Last! 57

1. A Hug for Pa

Inside our two-room cabin beside the rutty wagon road ma was cooking a hoecake of plain cornmeal and salt pork in the fireplace. Sassafras tea was boiling in an iron kettle.

Julie had already set up the dishpan on an empty flour barrel in a corner. It was her job to clean up after meals. With a homemade fork on a long wire handle, Nina was turning the meat. Ma kept me busy piling fresh wood on the fire, while the younger children crowded close to watch. We were all hoping pa would get home in time for breakfast.

"Charlie, please don't sweep so hard. You stir up too much dust while we're cooking," ma said patiently.

"That's twice ma asked you, Mr. Hard Head," Julie said. "You better listen."

"I'm not sweeping too hard, ma. This broom—"

"Brooms don't sweep by themselves," Nina scolded.

"All right now, children. You know what we believe—peace and quiet."

"Yes, ma," they said.

Ma turned to the others. "Emma, you and Elmira wash the little chaps' faces good and comb their hair." Our parents always called us chaps. "Hershey, you and Lester spread some cotton sacks to cover the splinters in the corner and sit the small ones near the fire."

"Yes, ma."

Ma never complained about the shabbiness of our home, which was a typical sharecropper's cabin in the Mississippi hills in 1915. Ours was a happy home because ma was so patient and kind. We adored her as much for her gentleness as for her beauty.

Her name was Tanna, and she was a mulatto, tall and round. She wore her honey-colored hair in plaits. Her skin was a soft, delicate hue. Her light-green eyes, always smiling, lent a gentle radiance to her face. Next to pa, who was a preacher, she was recognized as the best Bible scholar in the county. She taught Sunday school in pa's two small country churches, played the organ, and often led mid-week prayer services.

By the time I was ten, there were twelve of us children. I was tall for my age, ginger colored and brown eyed. Fourteen-year-old Emma was the eldest, Julie next, then Nina. The girls were tall and round like ma. They had jet-black hair and black eyes.

Charlie was a year younger than I. The others in order were Hershey, Lester, Elmira, Callie and Cardie who were twins, then Roni and Mattie.

Everyone scurried about doing the tasks ma had assigned. She said to me, "Son, go outside to fetch . . ." Then she stopped. "Oh I dropped the dishrag!"

"Dropping a dishrag means someone's coming hungry," piped Julie.

Ma giggled, "Hope it's pa."

"Me too."

I ran outside and looked up the road for pa.

I saw, instead, the chickens and the turkeys scratching for early morning breakfast. Our ducks and geese sailed on the pond. Some distance from the cabin, the hogs complained that they, too, wanted to be fed.

The sun, peeping over the treetops and the piney hills, shone into my eyes. I felt the sting of a chilly north wind. Over the open cotton, the brown cornstalks, and the green potato vines lay the sparkling dew.

I picked up an armful of wood and hurried back inside.

Suddenly, from where she was milking the cow, Em called, "Ma, pa's coming!"

Ma ran to the cracked mirror on the mantle and began to primp.

The children all teased, "Ma, you're pretty enough for pa. He'll be too glad to see you to notice how you look."

We knew she felt happy because she only answered, "Shucks!" Em ran through the back door with a huge bucket of milk as ma hurried out the front door to the yard. We followed her.

Pa was driving a twelve-yoke oxteam down the

long hill. We could see huge dark logs piled high on the long wagon.

We ran to greet pa, meeting him at the bottom of the hill.

Ma flew into pa's arms. We crowded about them, hoping pa would pat our heads. But he did more than pat. With his extra-long arms, he hugged us all—half at a time.

Pa was the Reverend James Streeter, but he was better known as "Big Preacher." The eldest son of his family, he stood over six feet tall and was built strong and heavy. Almost as black as tar, he had a huge head, black eyes, and large pearly white teeth. His face was strong and firm, but showed deep compassion.

The oxen did not seem to be interested in our happy greeting. With lowered heads and with steam pouring from their nostrils, the big beasts plodded into the yard.

Pa had left three weeks before, taking the ox-team to Chula where he helped to saw and fell many trees. This was the first load of logs.

"I'm glad to be back with you and the chaps," pa said to ma.

"We're proud to have you home again, pa," we chorused.

"The oxen yours, pa?" the twins asked.

"No. The logs and the team belong to our white boss man, Al Hill. He hires me to cut down the trees and drive them to his mill where he'll saw the logs into lumber. He's fixing to build more cabins for other field hands."

"Poor folks like us can't own that many oxen and a wagon," ma explained.

"When we get bigger, we'll help pa buy this team, won't we, chaps?" I asked.

"Yes," they chorused.

Suddenly ma screamed, "Son. The food's on the fire!"

I ran back to the cabin just in time to snatch the pan off the coals. Today we were so happy we didn't mind badly scorched food.

2. Run!

One Sunday night after church, we were sitting around the fire as we often did, talking and eating popcorn and roasted peanuts. Ma said, "That was a good service we had with you chaps singing so well."

"You played better than they sang," pa said with a grin.

We all laughed, but Nina shook her fist at pa in fun.

"Son, put some more wood on the fire," ma said. "This house is colder than the one we moved from. You think so, pa?"

"Sure is. Soon as I get a chance, I'll split some boards and nail up those cracks."

Our crumbling home was windowless with a wind-battered dirt chimney. Inside were three rickety iron beds with straw mattresses and wooden slats. We had two handmade chairs with torn cowhide bottoms. The other seats were wooden blocks.

"The last house didn't have so many cracks. Why did we move from there?" Julie asked.

Ma sighed. "Well, some white men just don't deal fairly with us. We keep trying to find a good man who will treat us right. We keep looking for land where we can make a big crop and clear enough money to buy a wagon and team. As long as we sharecrop, we'll likely keep moving. The year you were born, Son, we moved here to Pine Ridge."

"I'm proud that you are my mother. We can be happy anywhere with you and pa," I cried.

"We sure can," the others chimed in.

"Thanky. We still haven't found a place to live where we can get ahead. At least we are a fine family, all happy and healthy together."

"Amen!" pa said in a loud, deep voice.

We all burst out laughing.

He waved at the children. "Thank you chaps for a happy night. I think we'll go to bed now.

Want to be in the field early in the morning."

Ma nodded her approval.

"Want to finish picking cotton in a few weeks, so you chaps can go back to school this fall. Not another year is going by without you chaps in school, even though it is a long walk down out of these hills."

"We want to give you a good education so that you can make a better life than we have," ma breathed.

"Hallelujah!" pa murmured.

One Saturday afternoon that same fall, pa's parents, Jerry and Bertie, and pa's youngest sister, Alidee, came in a wagon to our cabin. When the greetings were over, grandma said, "See here, preacher, your brother Charlie sent these train tickets so we could go and stay with him awhile in Dallas, Texas."

"That's wonderful," pa said. "Charlie seems to be doing better than any of us."

"His letter says he owns a nice, big house. He wants us to take your younger chaps with us," grandma said.

Pa looked surprised at Charlie's suggestion.

"Oh, we can take them along, preacher. We'd like to keep the little chaps until you get better settled." Grandma glanced around the cabin. "We figure you'll be moving again!"

"But the chaps, ma. I—well—we'll miss—"

"Maybe your ma's right, preacher," ma said softly. I could see tears in her eyes.

"Sure, sure," grandma cried.

Pa gazed at ma. "Well, if you think so . . ."

Grandpa said, "We don't think. We know. We haven't reared our seventeen children just thinking."

"The Lord will bless you," ma said. Tears flowed down her cheeks.

Ma and the older girls bustled about helping the seven children who were leaving to dress in clean, patched clothes.

We hugged and kissed them, placed them in the wagon on old quilts and burlap sacks. We waved until the wagon rolled out of sight into the woods.

It was hard to see them go, but we didn't have long to feel lonely because of what happened soon after. Pa had walked fifteen miles to

the railroad town of Sidon in the Mississippi Delta to see about a job. He wanted to get away from sharecropping.

Before he left, he said, "Maybe this time I can make some good money and find a better place to live."

"That's wonderful. Thank you for your concern of us," ma answered.

The second day in that fall of 1915 after pa left, ma and I were sawing firewood in the front yard. It was growing dark.

"Sure do miss pa and the little ones," ma said wistfully. "Guess the chaps are in Dallas by now. But I'm proud the way you help me protect the family when pa's gone. You may be only eleven, but you already seem like a man."

"I'll always stand by you, ma," I answered solemnly.

We heard a rattling noise and looked up to see Al Hill driving up in his battered Ford pickup.

"Where's Big Preacher?" Al yelled from the truck.

"Gone to town," ma answered coldly.

Al said to me, "Give you a nickel, boy, if you fetch me a coal to light my pipe."

As I trotted toward the cabin, I heard him say to ma, "Come get the present I got for you here."

She was approaching the truck as I neared the cabin. When I came back outside with the fire, Al was grasping ma's arm.

"Take your hands off me!" she hissed. She jerked loose and nearly pulled Al out of the truck.

He jumped out and came toward her. Ma was furious now. He tried to grab her arm again, and I flung the fire away and dashed for the ax. Ma beat me to it. She snatched up the ax and nicked his arm.

Al bawled, "I'll get you!" Furious, he got into the pickup truck, but he couldn't get it started. While he cranked the motor, pa strode up the path out of the woods. He sensed at once that something terrible was wrong.

"What's the matter, Tan?" he asked.

I stared at ma. She didn't want pa to get into trouble. But she had to tell him the truth.

"Al tried to pull me into his truck." Her voice trembled.

Pa became so angry that he lunged for the man. "You—I'll break your neck with my bare hands!"

We knew he would too. We grabbed him, begging, "Pa, please, don't kill the man. His mob will get you."

The other children rushed out to help hold pa. He could have flung us away, but he didn't want to hurt us.

Finally, Al got the truck started and, looking scared, jumped in. As he drove off, he called back, "I'll kill you, Big Preacher. You can't hit a white man and get away with it."

"Pa, take ma where she'll be safe. Let me take care of the others," I pleaded. "I can do it the way you taught me. Send me word. We'll come to you. Go quick, pa."

"For our sake—for the children's sake, listen to him," ma cried.

"Pa, go!" I screamed.

Reluctantly, he yielded to our pleading, and together they slipped off into the forest.

3. On Our Own

It wasn't long before our food ran out. The snow had come early that year; although I had tried to hunt, I couldn't catch very much. The snow reminded me of the almanac. I took it off the mantle, and Em read it.

"My goodness," she exclaimed. "The almanac says this is to be the coldest winter in fifty years!"

"More snow will surely come," I added, "but we'll get along!"

We missed pa and ma terribly.

"You got to get us some grub, Son," Em told me.

"Maybe today," I promised them as I started out the door. "That snow will make it easier to find rabbits. Soon as I catch one, you can cook it good, Em."

"You never miss with your slingshot," Charlie boasted.

"Wait, Son! Ma would pray," piped Julie. "Our Father . . ."

We all knelt on our bare knees. ". . . who art in heaven . . ." Snow drifted through the large cracks in the roof and walls. Em was clad only in a tattered cotton-sacking dress. The others held burlap bags tight around their shoulders to keep warm. We all shivered as we prayed.

". . . give us . . . ," our teeth clicked, and our bodies quivered against the frigid air, ". . . this day our daily bread . . ."

I rose from my knees.

"Em, Al's been here twice with his gun—"

"Well, if he thinks he can scare us into telling him where pa is, he's wrong. We don't even know where pa is," she said. "He's taken the cows, the hogs, and the chickens for the money pa owes him. What do you think he'll do next?"

"I'm always afraid to leave you all," I said worriedly. "But I got to find food."

"We know. We'll watch for Al through the cracks. If we see him, we'll scream for you," Em promised. "I'll keep the ax handy. You go ahead."

I was already toughened to the misery, the hunger, and the poverty of the Mississippi hills. Dressed in dirty, ragged cotton-sacking shirt and pants, bareheaded and barefoot, I started out on the hunt. My long, kinky hair was matted with dirt and straw. My skin was blackened by the winter's biting wind. I was bony, stringy, and gaunt. I hadn't eaten for several days.

Crouching low, I crept across the snow-covered cotton field. My eyes darted from dried grass patch to dead stumps.

I was shivering, tears streamed down my cheeks, and my fingers were like ice sticks. I could hardly hold my slingshot. But I dared not risk the noise of beating my hands against my sides to keep them warm.

Then from under my cold-deadened feet, a huge rabbit darted from a patch of grass and streaked across the field. I staggered after it.

"Lord Jesus," I prayed, "don't let that rabbit get away!"

Over a hill and into a briar patch the rabbit ran. On hands and knees I crawled into the thicket. Every inch I moved, more angry barbs stuck into my flesh. When I wriggled up against a solid wall of briars, I could go no farther. I could see the rabbit's track where it had scurried under the cutting thorns. On each side of me the briars were so closely netted that I could not turn around. At last I backed out.

My arms and legs were stiff, and I had no feeling in my feet. But my will to get food and to survive gave me strength.

"Lord," I moaned, "help me find that rabbit."

I trotted about in search of signs of the hidden rabbit, but I could find none. Night began to close in. The wind howled as if calling up lost souls.

"Have mercy, L-o-r-d—" I began to pray. "Am I dying? I cannot feel myself. I cannot hear. I mustn't go to sleep." I stumbled and sprawled in the snow. I tried to cry out, but not even a whisper escaped my throat.

"Lord Jesus," I moaned, "don't let me die!"

I dug into the snow, trying to get up. Even

though my fingers were numb, they clutched an object that felt familiar. I clawed the object out of the snow. It was a huge ear of corn. My heart leaped with joy.

"Thanky, Jesus," I whispered.

With this new hope, my heart pounded with gladness and pumped blood through my cold-stiffened body. Staggering to my feet, I made my way toward home. By the time I reached the cabin, I felt a little stronger. Em helped me shed my wet rags and wrapped me in a quilt.

We were joyous over the food. Em shucked the corn, found it to be good, and shelled it. She then pounded it into a coarse meal, which she cooked into a mush. Before we began to eat, we all exclaimed together, "Thanky, Jesus. Thanky for our daily bread."

Next morning I was up before it was light. It was snowing again. With my slingshot and some rocks in hand, I slipped out the back door. My nerves were tight. A gust of wind almost knocked me down.

"Lord Jesus," I cried, "give me strength—"

I bent my bare head and plunged downwind.

The snow whirled, blinding me at times. But I went on for an hour or more.

"I'll get no rabbit today either," I moaned. "I better go back to the house before I freeze to death."

As I stumbled toward the shack, I *thought* I glimpsed a huge rabbit hopping in the snow. I was right—it was a real rabbit!

"The Lord will provide," I said with joy.

I began creeping toward the game.

It hopped around and faced me. I stood dead still and held my breath, as if the rabbit could hear me breathing above that roaring wind.

"Yes, sir, you are a rabbit-eating human. I'll run!" he seemed to say, and he bounced off across the field.

It was good luck that we were in an open field. That rabbit had a harder time fleeing in the deep snow than I had chasing him.

As I ran, I fitted a rock into my slingshot. By that time the rabbit ran onto a burned-over sage straw patch.

"Good Lord!" I thought. "I got a clear shot at last. Not too long. Thanky . . ."

I stopped. Two fast twirls over my shoulder, and "Swish!" snapped the slingshot.

I saw the rabbit leap into the air and then drop to the snow. I flew to the game and snatched it up.

Gladness poured strength into my legs, and I raced to the shack. Before I was inside the door, the other children leaped upon me. They bore me to the floor. They patted me and they kissed me.

"Son! Son! You've saved our lives!"

Soon Em sprang up and pulled the others off me. She and I dressed the game, and she boiled it in weakly salted water. We also saved the entrails, which she boiled separately.

"Wish ma and pa were here," I cried. "I'd sure like them to have some of this rabbit."

"Hope they in a good warm place," Em said.

"Where you suppose they are?" Julie asked.

"Jesus knows," put in Nina and Charlie.

We ate the whole rabbit and the entrails.

After we had finished, I put on a large back log and stoked the fire to keep all night. We curled up with our clothes on and slept.

4. The Dangerous Journey

Several nights after our parents had fled, the door suddenly flew open when we were asleep. We sat up, and to our horror we saw Al Hill in the doorway. He held a lantern high in one hand; in the other he gripped a repeating shotgun.

Behind Al we could see the dark outlines of three other men. They followed Al into the room. I recognized one as a kind man I'd met at the corn mill where I had worked.

My fighting instinct drove my hand to grab the handle of the razor-sharp ax, which I kept under the mattress at night.

"Get out of here!" I screamed, the sweat bursting out over me.

"Where's your pa hiding?" Al Hill snarled. We didn't answer.

He shifted the light to his gun hand. Then he snatched the mattress off the bed, spilling us onto the floor.

"You got him hid under there?" He kicked over the bed.

The man from the mill caught Al's arm, saying, "Just poor black kids. Not worth your trouble."

Al waved the others through the door and followed them.

I slammed the door shut and watched him through the cracks. With gun in hand, he crept to the corncrib to look for pa. He shoved the lantern into the crib and peered inside.

The man who had spoken to Al rushed back into the cabin to whisper to us, "Git! Right quick. I'll get him away from here now, but he'll be back. If he ever gets on your track, he'll hunt you as he would an animal!"

He hurried to the pickup truck waiting on the snow-covered dirt road.

Al soon joined them, and they drove off.

"Let's git!" I said. "You chaps help me pack."

We dumped our meager possessions into cotton sacks and two burlap bags. I would carry the tin dishes, a small bucket of salt, one small iron pot, and an iron skillet. I had spent a great deal of time in the woods, and I knew what we'd need for traveling on foot in the vast forest. Divided among the others were more sacks, two plow lines, the ragged quilts, and the *Black Draught Almanac*. Pa had taken the Bible, which was the only other book in the cabin.

We also had a five-gallon iron pot with an iron handle and a top which was ventilated with four holes. For several years ma had used the pot to carry fire to the field when we picked cotton on the frozen ground. To carry the pot we had a long, stout iron rod, thickly padded at each end to rest on the shoulders. Pa had screwed two u–bolts about an inch apart around the middle of the rod to keep the pot from sliding.

With a strong wire I fastened the ax to the rod. Then I stuck the rod through the handle of the pot to lift to our shoulders.

We tied on the burlap shoes which the girls

had made and lashed extra cotton sacks around us. I filled the pot with good coals and a small block of wood. We must carry fire with us, or we might freeze if our clothing got wet.

Em and I lifted the rod with the pot to our shoulders.

"Keep quiet!" I whispered.

"Sure will," she said.

Soon we were in the woods of giant oaks and pines. I knew the whirling snow would quickly cover our tracks as the wind began to rise.

We were soon exhausted. To help, I lashed the others together with the ropes and looped one end over my shoulder. Into the ear of each I whispered encouragement. "We're going to pa and ma."

"Where?" Charlie asked.

"I have a feeling where to go. My faith is leading us to them—due east."

"How far?" Julie and Nina wanted to know.

"Long way. We'll make it," I assured them.

The going was slow and hard. We stopped to

rebuild the pot fire and warm ourselves, but we tramped all night.

Then came the frigid morning. Exhausted, wet, and cold, we stumbled upon a large brush pile of young pines and cedars. I gathered hardwood and fat pine and replenished our firepot. Then I pushed a hole under the brush pile for shelter. We would be safe for a time.

We were used to going hungry, so we slept all day.

"We got to eat!" I told Em, who was rubbing sleep from her eyes.

"Hope you get something, Son."

With the slingshot and the ax, I crept out from beneath the brush. The snow had stopped. Lord Jesus! What is that? I thought to myself. There on a low branch of a tree two dazzling balls of light glared at me.

Holding my breath, I eased the ax down and loaded the slingshot. I gave the sling three fast whirls. Then I loosed the rock with all of the power of my young muscles.

With a loud *rruummppp,* the balls flew out. There followed a muffled thud in the snow. I plowed through the snow and snatched up my prize. Wild turkey, maybe, I guessed.

Back under the brush with the kill, I wakened Em, who had dozed off. "Light a torch, girl," I whispered. "I got eats."

"W—what?" Em held up the torch.

The others woke then. "Je-sus—boy. An owl!"

After Em and I cleaned the owl, she boiled it about an hour. The entrails she cooked separately. Still it was hard meat to fight. Em saved some for later.

After we'd all eaten, I cautioned the others. "When we start out, there will be sinkholes in our path. Remember what I have taught you."

I put a small block of fat pine in the firepot. We crawled out to start tramping again. At intervals we rested to rebuild the fire and hover tight around it. We'd nibble a few bites at a stop.

By daylight we were in larger timber. As we pushed on, a cold, heavy rain began to stream off the trees. We were soaked and almost frozen. Our teeth chattered. We finally came out of the tall timber into a thick grove of short pine and cedar bushes.

Lighting a pine torch, I crawled through to the center of a cluster. The ground was dry. I pushed out, and we brought in our gear. The refuge warmed quickly and we dried.

"We've eaten the last of brother owl," Julie said.

"Maybe he got a free-hearted sister," Nina suggested.

"There is food, and Son will find it," Em said hopefully.

"I'm so hungry," moaned Julie.

"I'm hungry too, but it would be dangerous to leave you alone to go hunting in the daylight," I said. "Al might have reported to the sheriff that we're missing. The sheriff could be after us right now."

"Think the sheriff will really look for us in this forest?" Em asked.

"What if he catches us?" Julie questioned.

"Well, Al could report that pa threatened to kill him. The sheriff could put us in jail to try to force us to tell him where pa is," I explained.

"How long could he keep us in jail?" the children asked.

"Till he can notify our kinfolk to get us."

"You scared, Son? If you aren't, we aren't either."

I knew better than to tell them I was afraid. So, remembering ma's faith, I answered, "The Lord is our help."

Afterward I killed a coon which filled us. Em saved some for later.

The next afternoon the barking of hounds cut through our shelter. Rapidly the barking grew louder and drew nearer.

We peeped out in time to see a huge deer leaping by. Seconds later the yapping hounds raced after him. We'd scarcely covered the fire to hide the light when some men on horseback burst into view, whooping to the dogs.

Before the hunters were out of sight, I began to worry about our next move. I decided to wait for night again.

As darkness came, we packed and quickly started eastward. Much of the snow had melted. What remained had frozen hard. We hit giant timber with thick vines and underbrush. But we pushed on for we were too scared to stop.

5. Winter Camp

Splash! I dropped into a sinkhole. The rod slipped off Em's shoulder, and the coals spilled into the water. The fire sputtered and died. The children pulled me out. I was soaked from feet to head and fast chilling.

Charlie threw sacks around me, and I slipped out of my freezing rags. Em banged a skillet and the small pot together over a piece of quilt. The sparks soon ignited the piece. Julie cut some bigger kindling. When the fire was blazing in the pot, the others formed a tent with sacks, standing inside and under it. We huddled tight to the flames until we were warm.

Later the girls cut a pile of wood and soon had a log fire roaring.

"If the hunters see the fire, they'll think we are 'bad men' making whiskey secretly, and be scared to come up," I said. I wanted to drive away our fear. "Pa said whiskey makers will shoot you on the spot."

Em hung my stiff rags onto a bush close to the fire. She divided small portions of the meat, and we munched it.

After my clothes had dried, we pushed off. We came out of the forest at a dirt road. Across the road was a large cornfield. And beyond that open space, we could see the dark outline of some tall trees.

We had struck across the road into the field when a familiar shape caught my eye. "Someone forgot this basket," I said. "Lord Jesus. Corn!"

The others clustered around. "Bread!" they screamed.

We threw the corn into a sack and hung it on the rod. Then we plodded on across the field to the thick woods on the other side.

Late in the afternoon, we came out on a large plateau of tall slender pines. The trees had been slashed three or four years before, probably for a turpentine mill somewhere.

"Em—Julie—Nina—Charlie. I've been here before. Came with pa."

"Can you find a good place to rest a long—long—?" Em asked.

"A fox can find shelter. I'm wiser than a fox," I boasted. "I'll get food too. Look at the blackbirds."

We rambled about among a thick stand of cedar, pine, and holly bushes. We found several small rotten frame huts with warped and rust-eaten tin roofs. Next, almost hidden by rattan vines and bramble briars, we discovered a small solid log hut with no chimney.

"Thanks, Jesus!" exclaimed the others.

Holding a torch in one hand, I pushed a hole in the underbrush with the ax. Then I crept cautiously through the open door. Fluttering and squeaking bats streaked over my head.

The others cried out with fright.

"Just bats!" I called. The hut was full of

spider webs, bird droppings, and dirt. "Come. Clean up. Quick!" I urged.

I built a large dirt mound in the middle of the floor. We set the firepot on top. Em started the fire, while I scouted for water.

I found an old artesian well close by.

Soon I discovered a good plank. The girls scrubbed and washed it clean. Em would beat some corn into meal on it.

"I'm going to fetch some meat. You keep quiet!" I commanded. Going a short way, I saw a flock of blackbirds.

"Lord Je—sus!" Pa had taught me to make a game trap. I gathered some planks and hurried back to the hut.

"A thousand birds out there!" I cried.

"Lord, we eat bird pie," the others piped.

Together we constructed a long, shallow box with a detached floor. We also made a sliding door across one end. I had to make a pulley. Two ropes tied together would work. I nailed one end to the door.

A bush had grown up in the hut, and I cut it off. Then Em and I carried the trap and some

shelled corn and a burlap sack outside. We crept to the trees close to where the birds were flocking and set the trap. Using the bush to hide me as I moved, I dropped a line of corn between the birds and the trap door. Em sprinkled a handful inside. We slid behind a tree. I sent Em back to the hut, then I waited.

Finally one bird pecked the first grain of corn in the line. His friends joined him. The line marched to the trap door. The leader hopped in, and soon the trap was full.

Slap! I jerked the rope, and the door shut.

"Thanky, Jesus," I murmured. I carefully caught the live birds one by one and popped them into the sack. I ran back to the hut. We burst out laughing and crying over the catch. When we had calmed down, I told them, "Maybe we can stay until spring."

"How many, Son?" Charlie cried.

"Let's count," I replied. There were 27! We couldn't eat them all at once. I eased several cedar branches through some of the small holes in the burlap sack. This gave the birds walking space.

"We got to feed them too, until we can eat them," I said. Charlie helped me make a large tin cage, and we managed to feed and water all that I caught.

Later we searched for hunting tools. Rocks would serve in the slingshot. Small hickory would make a bow. Solid boards could be fashioned into arrows. In one shack I found a file and two sound bed slats. Under one floor I discovered some rocks.

I sharpened the pocketknife and the ax. I made arrows with the slats. Next, I fashioned points out of nails. I also made a bow from a small hickory and a piece of rope.

The sight and the scent of man moved the game away from us. I had to hunt farther from the hut. Still I managed to keep a small reserve of animals and birds.

One day I stumbled upon a dust-covered box in a shanty. Inside, school books, magazines, and newspapers greeted me! My find brought new life to us. "Now we can learn!"

6. We Must Go East

We spent the long afternoons reading and telling riddles. "When we see ma and pa again, we'll be educated," we boasted.

We read about Columbus, Ponce de Leon, De Soto, Captain John Smith, as well as George Washington and other presidents. We also read the almanac.

We loved the old riddles.

"What's this? Round as a saucer and deep as a cup. All King George's men can't pull it up?" asked Em.

We tried and tried. We gave up.

"A well!" she piped.

We rolled all over the floor and laughed.

"All right, Miss Wise Em. Top this. Say right fast—six slick ships slicked sliding six city biscuits!"

"Ships—six—no—biscuits—slicked—" She gave up. We would roll and kick and laugh with tears streaming.

Spring came to float quietly over the forest. The trees unfolded their green cloaks. Grass, weeds, and flowers discarded their winter blankets. It was time to go because Wisdom again was whispering to me with that feeling, with that faith, "Come east, Son. Come east."

"It's safe to leave now," I told the others. "Hunters quit the woods until winter. If lawmen are searching for us, they are mounted. They'll never ride their horses in this forest at night, because there are too many sinkholes." I waved toward thicker woods. "Quicksand and marshes are along all the creeks."

"Think the sheriff's still looking for us, Son?" Em asked anxiously.

"If Al still wants revenge on pa, he'll tell the law to keep looking for us. The sheriff will call other lawmen in several counties, giving them our description. Pa said the sheriff gets a fee for every person he arrests."

"If the sheriff does find us, he'll get five fees, enough to buy his wife a dress," Julie added.

We burst out laughing.

"We'll travel by night, rest by day," I decided.

I had already cured three coons for the trip. Em now broiled enough birds to last several days. I set the rest of the creatures free. A few birds and two young coons refused to leave! They followed us toward hard timber.

Wisdom seemed to speak silently to me more often now. It seemed that I heard the voice say, "Your journey shall grow harder. You will meet a person who will direct you to your parents." It was not a voice. Rather, it was a feeling—a steadfast hope, a faith.

With torches to light our path, we plodded at night over hills and down into valleys. Often we would stop to rest and to eat. Then we'd push on to skirt lakes and ford shallow creeks. Because hunting season had passed, I had to kill half-grown rabbits and wild young pullets for food. The coons clung to us. Usually, however, they caught their own lizards and scorpions. The forest blazed with the blooms of wild flowers and wild fruit.

Early one night we hit a lowland and had to stop. The others slept, but I stayed awake, for in the bright light of the moon we could see small lakes. And in the shallows, the shapes of turtles and huge snakes filled us with dread. We would have to travel by day now, so we could see the creatures in the bushes along the shore.

We skirted the lakes to come to what seemed to be a long, huge Indian mound through a small timberland. Next morning we struck marsh land. Again we must go slowly. I knew certain death waited there in beds of quicksand covered with tall grass. We tramped first east and then north. We could find no way to cross the marsh.

Again came that faith when Wisdom seemed to whisper to me, "Go south . . ."

I frowned, but I could not question Wisdom. We plodded on. We ran onto a long ridge about ten or twelve feet high above the marsh. By that time a soft rain was falling. Suddenly we came right upon a long, wide lake. We could not see the outline of trees on the other shore because of a heavy mist.

"We'll have to make a raft somehow," I told Em.

"Ma would pray, Son. Let's kneel." And there we knelt while Em prayed, "Our Father who art in heaven . . ."

We had some wood and fat pine. By nightfall we managed to cut two dogwood trees, scores of rattan vines, and a few poles. We dragged them to the lake shore. I shot two ducks and a crane. We ate the ducks, and the coons ate the crane.

We had to wait for daylight. And we kept a torch burning all night.

With daybreak, we saw that dark clouds hung low. Fog was so thick that we could almost dip it with a bucket. After dragging the trees into the water, we lashed them together with the vines. We then loaded the coons. Our birds came to perch on the raft.

In that fog I was afraid to land, because I didn't know whether or not the marsh surrounded the lake. To land in the marsh might

mean death to us all. I could not risk it. So we drifted all day.

Next morning the fog lifted slowly. Soon the sun marched hot and bright. Often the coons snatched up tiny water creatures.

At last we came out on a sandbar. Laughing and crying aloud for joy, we scrambled ashore. "Thanky, Jesus. Thanky!"

Soon Wisdom said in a feeling, not a voice, "Come east!" We crawled up high hills and slid down into deep valleys. We were silent and so tired. The only sound was our footsteps squashing on the leaves and the spongy earth.

Again the feeling came through to me: "Come up the hill."

When we reached the top, before us stood a tall, slender, jet-black woman with black hair flowing loose. Her eyes were dark and piercing. She was carrying a basket of dewberries, and she beckoned us to follow her.

7. Together at Last!

The woman walked eastward deep into the woods. We trailed after her. When we reached her log house, she said in a soft voice, "Rest your things. I'm Mrs. Yadi Zion of the Holy Train which has brought you here. You are James, called Son."

She nodded to the others, "And you are Emma—Julie—Nina—Charlie." She even told us our ages. Then she sent the girls into the front room, us boys into the back.

"Right now, bathe."

Wooden tubs, towels, soap, and homemade nightclothes were laid out in our rooms. She had brought hot water.

After we had bathed, she fed us home-cured ham, bacon, eggs, biscuits, jam, and buttermilk.

"Go feed the pets, Son," Mrs. Zion directed. "After you all rest, I shall tell you why you came here."

I did not know how long we slept. But, as if she knew the minute we'd waken, she had set a hot dinner on the table. We came out on the porch in the clothes she had made for us.

After we'd washed, she beckoned us into the dining room. We ate canned vegetables—corn, tomatoes, string beans—and corn bread, and drank lemonade. I fed our little friends again.

When we'd finished, she led us out to the front yard. We sat on the grass under a cherry tree, while she told us this exciting story:

Her husband was the inspector of much of that timberland through which we had come. The young white woman who owned the property was a descendant of a clan who had settled there in the 1700s. Those people had also owned Yadi's ancestors, who in time had bought their freedom.

Once free, the Zions set up an organization

called the Holy Train, which helped escaped slaves to freedom. The Holy Train had been active ever since. Now it helped black people who had been unjustly imprisoned to escape. It also saved many from lynching. One most important belief was that each officer of the Train must be holy. He must know the past, the present, and the future. He must be able to talk to people, even some thousands of miles away, through the Mind.

Mrs. Zion was president of the Holy Train. Her home was the headquarters. My parents had gone to her to ask her to bring us there. Through Mind she and other members of the Holy Train had guided ma and pa to safety. She had contacted me that night when Al Hill came to our cabin.

About midnight on a Monday, she woke us, saying, "Arise. Eat a big supper." She then gave us a basket of food. By that time two huge black men drove up in a spring wagon.

"Go with them," Mrs. Zion told us. "They belong to the Holy Train. They'll start you on your way to your parents."

So from Holy Station to Holy Station we rode. At times we were in buggies, in trucks, or on horseback. As the cocks crowed for another Monday, we reached our parents' home in the Tennessee mountains.

Ma and pa were standing on the porch because they were expecting us. As we approached the pasture gate nearly a quarter mile from the house, they ran down the road to meet us. We hopped out of the wagon and into their arms.

Ma cried with unrestrained joy, "I thank thee, O heavenly Father, because thou hast heard me." She kissed us as if we were just born.

I knew that pa was a giant, but I had never felt that strength until then. I screamed out because he hugged me so tight. He kissed the girls as if they were babies.

The Holy Men then drove us to the house. Ma and pa invited them in, but they politely declined. They said they had to rescue other people soon. They hurried down the road.

Our parents told us that through Mind, Mrs. Zion had often talked with them about us. She always told them the truth concerning where we

were and also how we were. If we were cold, wet, and hungry, she informed them of that. But she always assured them that we would be all right.

She also promised that in due time she would deliver us to them well dressed, fed, and healthy.

Ma and pa said that they had worked and saved to be ready when we came.

"The voice, Faith, said you'd be here today," ma said with a laugh. "So we prepared—" pa began, but checked himself, glancing at ma.

They told us of their journey here. They'd gone by the home of a friend. He'd given pa a rifle, some ammunition, and food. The woman had given ma some clothes.

Being an expert woodsman and a strong man, pa took ma on the long trip through the forests without too much trouble. They knew Mrs. Zion, and they went to see her and ask her to send us to them.

The story finished, they took us into the other room. On the bed were piles of new clothes for all of us. We hugged and kissed our parents. We sat on the floor and cried with joy.

Ma backed into the kitchen, beckoning to us. We followed on all fours. We shook the kitchen with shouts of laughter. We clapped our hands and hopped up and down. Our pet coons hid from the noise behind the door.

"God has brought you safely home. So here's the feast," pa crowed.

On the long table were a roasted pig, two roasted chickens, and two roasted ducks. There were also cakes, pies, corn bread, and biscuits.

We children knelt, and Em prayed.

Pa had to work days in a distant logging camp. But he had walked back home the night we got there to talk with us.

"Son," he began, and his voice trembled, "I don't want to move but one more time—to Wewoka, Oklahoma. That's where our old friend Brother Flemming and his family have gone. Then I want to give you chaps a good home and a fine education."

Ma nodded and smiled. "And soon we'll bring the little chaps home from Texas. We'll all be together again."

That year we all worked hard to make money

and save it for our move West. Pa took care of the crops. Ma and the girls took in washing and ironing. I helped pa and caught fish and killed game.

Pa was so proud of us all! The day I came home with money from furs I'd sold, pa beamed on me and I felt nine feet tall. A real man at eleven—going on twelve—that's what I was.

But the money was slow coming in, and finally we decided it was best for pa to take what we had and go ahead West. Maybe he could do better out there.

We felt sad to break up the family again, but ma had faith we'd somehow get enough money together to follow pa soon.

It took a year of hard work and the help of a kind friend to bring that glad day. When it came, we didn't know whether to laugh or cry, so we did both and then we offered a prayer of thanks.

The very next morning we shut the cabin door for the last time. Then ma led off with a hymn, and we all joined in as we headed for the train that would carry us to pa in Indian Territory.